BMW CLASSICS

BMW CLASSICS

Jeremy Walton

Published in Great Britain in 1994 by Osprey,
an imprint of Reed Consumer Books Limited,
Michelin House, 81 Fulham Road, London
SW3 6RB and Auckland, Melbourne, Singapore
and Toronto

ISBN 1 85532 329 X

Editor Shaun Barrington
Page design Paul Kime/Ward Peacock
Partnership
Printed in Hong Kong

Title page
*BMW four cylinder HQ, Munich,
towering above the BMW-embossed
museum. There are other BMW sites
scattered across the city*

Front cover
*The Munich factory owned 327 coupé
shows photographer Andrew Yeadon
how BMW established their reputation
for elegant bodywork in association with
the coachwork specialists of the thirties*

Back cover
*The variety of BMWs with classic appeal
is apparent from this Peter Osborne
group picture of: (left to right) 1980
mid-engine M1, the almost as rare Glas-
BMW 1600 GT, the 2500 saloon, 2002
turbo and 3.2 litre CSL coupé. Cars,
courtesy of L&C, Tunbridge Wells*

For a catalogue of all books published by Osprey Automotive
please write to:

**The Marketing Department, Reed Consumer Books,
1st Floor, Michelin House, 81 Fulham Road, London SW3 6RB**

About the author

Jeremy Walton was 46 when this, his 21st book, was published. He had previously written four BMW titles and translated a company history. Walton's 1979 Osprey title, *Unbeatable BMW* is now regarded as a collector's out-of-print classic in the USA and UK, changing hands at more than five times the original list price.

Acknowledgements

This book was created to meet a concept from Tony Holmes and Shaun Barrington at Osprey. I cannot pretend Colin Burham's camera expertise, but his example inspired me to try the USA as a backdrop.

My thanks to Travelwright in Henley-on-Thames (especially to Keith J. Wright for a superb USAir/Hertz itinerary at short notice), thanks made poignant because Keith Wright was fighting a battle against cancer, one that he subsequently lost.

This book could not have been completed without the enthusiasm of Richard Conway at RC Motorsports, North Carolina. Encouragement also came from BMW of North America, particularly employees Erik C. Wensberg (Promotions Manager) and Event Marketing Manager, Gerry Bill.

In the UK thanks to Tim Hignett of the L&C BMW dealership, Tunbridge Wells, Kent, for filling photographic gaps with an outstanding collection of modern BMW classics. A smaller private selection was provided by British BMW loyalist Neville Hay and family. I was also treated with maximum cooperation by Graham Arnold and Susan Hicks, joint organisers of the BMW Exhibition-92 at Stonleigh, Warwickshire, through their independent outfit: BMW Drivers Car Club. The few factory collection pictures we reproduce came from BMW (GB) Ltd in association with photographer Andrew Yeadon. Thanks also to Andrew Morland for photographic input.

The 35 mm pictures were mostly taken by the author for this title using a 1979 Canon AE-1 and a Pentax PC35AF. Film was 90 per cent FujiChrome, processing by Kodak. The L&C dealership collection pictures were augmented by a professional photographer friend, Peter Osborne. Peter used a Bronica 2. 25" camera and Fujichrome.

Introduction

This book marks a personal first. Although I have written about BMW in books and magazines many times, I have never been entrusted with the photographic side of the subject before. One glance at the pictures may tell you why this has been the case ... However, Osprey are professionals who will have filtered out 99 per cent of the intrusive tree trunks and lampposts that I captured.

The challenge was simple, but expensive. Dare to take on this project, and there had to be pictures. Good pictures, but above all original, personal, pictures. The brief was concise: "we're not interested in old handouts and press pack stuff. We don't care how you do it, but be back here in three months with some material we can all be proud of".

Richard Conway, for RC Motorsports in North Carolina, USA had written to me early in 1992. Richard previewed a 20 year celebration that was planned for Florida during November 1992 and the annual BMW Car Club (North America) Oktoberfest.

Less than a fortnight remained before that festival took place when I decided to go. I shut my eyes and put my Barclaycard to the sword, arriving on the second morning of that five day American celebration.

Since BMW Car Club has over 28,000 members in the USA, I expected something special. It was. I will not forget the magnificent displays, or the kindness shown to me, particularly by the 500 guests assembled by the club and BMW North America Inc for the dinner. I acted as MC to a dramatic evening of fun (assisted by David Hobbs, Sam Posey, Dieter Quester and Brian Redman) and history; for it was here that Marc Surer announced a BMW withdrawal from the 1993 Deutsche Rennmeisterschaft racing series.

That may seem a glossy and unrelated feast to the business of grass roots BMW motoring, such as running a classic 2002 on a tight budget. Not so. America opened my eyes to the greatest enthusiasm for the product I have seen. I learned a lot about keeping a modern classic in America, and a lot more about improving its daily practicality, especially from those in the northern states who build from scratch sometimes. These are people who are not afraid to raid other manufacturer's parts stores to locate a cheaper item of equal durability and increased efficiency.

The choice of material was entirely mine. There will be BMW purists who will shake their heads sadly, for this book is not an essay into the finer points of esoteric rarities or history. My enthusiasm is for spreading the word that BMW admiration, or ownership, need not be an elitist activity.

I also do not think that the abused definition 'classic' has to be applied only to an obsolete machine. A seventh edition of The Concise Oxford Dictionary makes its first definition choice of the term classic as, 'of the first class, of acknowledged excellence, remarkably typical, outstandingly important'. The Oxford editors add the reminder that classic style means, 'simple, harmonious, well proportioned and finished, in accordance with established forms'.

That is why I have paid such special attention to BMW's role in creating coupés, devices that sell primarily on form, regardless of the year of manufacture. I am a devoted fan of the current 3-series coupé, believing it to be the true inheritor of the accessible CSi/CSL legend, which harks back to the virtually unobtainable strata of the fifties 503/507 V8s.

More than twenty years ago, I drove a BMW 3-litre CS in the annual Belgian Spa-24 hour classic race. I hope that the pleasure and 'special place' BMW has had in my heart since that adventure will be apparent in this book and that some of the sheer enjoyment will be shared by the reader.

Jeremy Walton
Henley-on-Thames, England

Right
1939 BMW328; an unmatched power-to-weight ratio, and surely an inspiration for the post-war Jaguar XK

Contents

Roots

The birth of the BMW we know today is a fascinating tale, one strewn across two World Wars and the reunification of Germany. It has its roots beyond the turn of the century: 3 December 1896, to be precise. That was the point at which recognisable Wartburg of Eisenach (within what was to be East Germany) company strands weave a story that encompasses period names – Fahrzeugfabrik Eisenach, Rapp Motorenwerken GmbH, Cyklon, Wartburg and Dixi – in equally unlikely activities.

Everything from military hardware to railway braking systems, powered mountain bikes and saucepan manufacture has a place in a full history of Bayerische Motoren Werke: Bavarian Motor Works, usually contracted to BMW. From the start BMW history is packed with strong personalities (particularly inventors and financiers), who have achieved considerable competitive success. Their creative endeavour found expression in armaments, aviation and marine power units. But it was primarily the manufacture of motorcycles that led to the best known BMW products – automobiles.

The famous BMW initials were first derived from an aeroplane engine manufacturing concern, one registered 7 March 1916, the official company birthday, although the whirling propeller emblem was not registered until October 1917. Towards the end of World War I BMW were commissioned with an order for 2,000 Type IIIa aero motors. These were of an inline six layout that was already testing (September) and flying (November) in 1917. The unit went on to the aeronautical Hall of Fame, pulling an average 185 bhp for first World War German fighter pilot aces such as Ernst Udet and 'Top Gun' Baron Manfred Freiherr von Richthofen (aka: 'The Red Baron').

The BMW symbol was created at the behest of Franz Joseph Popp, board director and BMW chief engineer who had persuaded the embryo BMW into manufacturing an Austro-Daimler aero engine under licence. Popp had a strong alliance with former Mercedes design engineer, Dr Max Friz (1914 Grand Prix motor designer) who had also worked on the first military aero motor for Daimler.

For much of BMW's history there is surprisingly little interaction between bikes and cars, or cars and aviation, although it was originally intended to stand on these 'three legs'.

Motorcycles came first, with aero engine designer Max Friz creating the first of the twin opposed cylinder engines, more often known as 'Boxer' units after the cross-punching style of their horizontal pistons and connecting rods. The first BMW 500cc twins were powering production R32 motorcycles by 1923.

Car manufacture remained a BMW ambition, even after 1922 had seen the Allies lift the official ban on German assembly of aeroplane engines with a consequent lift to complex company fortunes. BMW has remained at the

Above right
The beginnings of both BMW's reputation for inline six cylinder sporting products, and serious motor sporting success, came with the 1934–36 open two seater, 315/1. The 1.5 litre wore triple Solex carburettors, developed 40 bhp and could exceed 70 mph

Right
The saloon car origins of the 315/1 are betrayed by the large VDO clock to match the speedometer, rather than the traditional large scale tachometer

Left

Nierenformig, the kidney-shaped grille pattern, came to BMW on the 1933 saloon, 303, which also debuted their love affair with inline six cylinder engines. Here is the classic rendition, as featured on the magnificent 328 of Richard Matorell in the USA

Above

Forever BMW in the German public perception: the full frontal view of the gracious factory 327 coupé

forefront of the aviation engine business, although today's power units are bred in association with Rolls Royce.

Following some false starts with a Dr Ferdinand Porsche sports prototype (Sascha) and an aerodynamic front drive design (three prototypes, badged SHW, were made), early company history allied Britain and Germany. Inspired dealing from Italian Camillo Castiglioni (a central figure in BMW's early, and often precarious, financial affairs) brought BMW the Dixi (née Wartburg) company at Eisenach on 1 October 1928; with that deal came the licensed right to assemble the Dixi 3/15 (Austin Seven).

The 'Seven' proved a very adaptable small car – it was also produced as far afield as Japan and the USA, as well as in Belgium and France – and one ideally suited to the worldwide depression that followed Wall Street's Black Friday (24 October 1929). BMW put their badge on the Dixi to enter car production in April 1929.

Their imaginative sales methods, including hire purchase, reaped considerable rewards. When BMW abandoned the basic 3/15 and Seven concept (749cc, with 15–18 bhp, delivering just 47–53 mph and 43–mpg) they

Spot the differences: Left and righthand drive 328 fascias. Seen at rest in Moroso Park Florida (LHD) and a Kentish country house for the RHD layout with German labled instruments

had sold 15,948 copies between 1929 and 1932. BMW also wafted out of the Austin agreement in a hurry (1 March 1932) having made many more of the sidevalve four cylinders than originally anticipated. Not all were immediately recognisable as BMWs, for the company also used the Wartburg name plate honourably on the pretty boat tail DA3 two seater of 1930.

Expansion in the Thirties

The Thirties marked BMW's rapid growth into the status of an established automobile manufacturer, but their four wheeler prowess was based at Eisenach, not Munich. Cars were to prove a mere a spot on the balance sheet compared with the impact of aero engine engineering on their labour and turnover statistics, centred at Munich.

BMW virtually doubled the work force – from 2800 to 4700 – in just one year (1932–33) and the gathering force of German nationalism propelled that employment figure to 12,500 by 1934. The overall trend was maintained too, BMW had no less than 47,300 deployed in the third year of World War II. Then the BMW 801 air-cooled radial motor series was selected for the Focke Wulf Fw 190A fighter, the prototype of which made its maiden flight at Bremen

Airport in 1939. Incidentally, the aircraft's first flight took place in full public view before the outbreak of WW2, yet amazingly this monumental event was completely missed by British intelligence. The Fw 190 came as a nasty shock to the RAF when it entered Luftwaffe service in the summer of 1941, outclassing the Rolls-Royce Merlin 45/46-powered Spitfire Mk V. Rated at 1700 hp for take-off, the 14-cylinder BMW 801 was significantly later in development and about 60 per cent bigger than the liquid-cooled V12 Merlin, and its remarkably neat installation in the Fw 190 virtually eliminated the frontal-area drag penalty normally associated with bulky air-cooled aero engines. A contemporary Royal Navy (Fleet Air Arm) test pilot's account of flying a captured Fw 190A-4 unwittingly added to the BMW legend. Captain Eric Brown commented of the 801D: 'We found that the BMW almost invariably fired first time and emitted a smooth purr as it ran'.

Back on the ground, BMW worked through the thirties to produce their own 'grown up' version of the Seven with a longer stroke engine (782 cc/20 bhp at 3500 rpm) which also had overhead valve operation and two roller bearings for the crankshaft. The 1932–34 AM-prefixed (Auto Munchen, Munich being the official company HQ and centre for engines engineering) 3/20 series (the first 3-series, if you like) sold more than 7,000 copies. Some are hard to identify, special coach built bodies being a feature of this European period.

For example, Mercedes at Sindelfingen made a variety of open and closed 3/20s. These two great German companies have cooperated (especially in the aero engine field) to a surprising degree. So now, when rivalries are so fierce, both commercially (1992 was the first year BMW made more cars than Mercedes) and in motor sports.

Students of the classic BMW form will probably note 1933 as the starting point for the company's step into inline six cylinder engine manufacture. The overhead valve sextets were first shown at Berlin in February 1933 in the shape of the 303 and had a clear bore and stroke ancestry deriving from their four cylinder forerunners. Yet they marked a new departure for BMW, one that was unable to mature fully before World War 2 interrupted its progression.

British 328 owner Tim Hignett of L&C BMW at Tunbridge Wells had owned this RHD example for three years when he not only allowed this photography session, but let the author drive his car as well. Now I know why Tim is so cheerful, for this machine delivers a unique motoring experience, one blending delicacy with speed in a fashion that only old Lotus models exhibit, and then without the fabled durability of this 1937–39 wonder. The white BMW, restricted steering lock and all, binds its fortunate driver to the 328 cause forever. Despite appearances, this RHD 328 was not one of the AFN BMWs that were so significant to UK sales, but came into Britain via the USA. It has also been displayed at the Frankfurt Motor Show on the BMW Ag stand

Nevertheless, the key 303 elements were there for postwar generations: The six cylinder engine of 30 bhp was to be the basis of a development programme that would yield important BMW and Bristol descendants, whilst the Nierformig (kidney-shaped) grille has been 'shrink-wrapped' to preserve its emotive appeal over 60 years.

The Classic 300s

The then contemporary four cylinder (309) marked the beginning of BMW badging logic, the '3' series followed by 09 for the 0.9 litre capacity (actually 845cc) in similar manner to the present BMW shorthand that gives us model line followed by cubic capacity in litres (for example 750 equals 7-series of 5-litres). In the thirties there were plenty of exceptions to this rule and American readers will know that they have had many more modern exceptions for emissions test reasons. These have included a 1981 model year '320i' that was actually a 1.8 litre of 318i stock.

Still the BMW badging generalisation stands; back in the thirties we find it fulfilled with the developing '300' line. The first sporting six cylinder BMWs of 1934–37 saw the 315 with longer stroke 1. 5 litre sixes as the first BMW saloons to storm the infant autobahnen systems at more than 100 km/h (62 mph). A 315 saloon offered twin Solexes, 5.6:1 compression ratio and 34 bhp.

Its 315/1 two seater cousin provided triple carburettors and an elevated 6. 8: 1 compression allowed 40 bhp and 75 mph for road customers. For BMW it gave them the first intoxicating taste of four wheeled motor sport success with their own designs (particularly for the Alpine Rally and Nurburgring sports car races), but company history also claims sporting victories from the Wartburg era.

The 315 had a bigger brother that also followed badge logic, the 319 having 1911cc that delivered more than 80 mph in the 319/1 sport (triple carburettor, high compression) guise. A cylinder bore increase of just 1 mm brought the most revered prewar BMW motor car engine closer to realisation: the 320 of 1937 powered by a 1971cc (66 × 96mm) unit of 'only' 45 bhp in saloon trim.

Logic was abandoned for the sequence of 321, 326, 327, 327/28 and legendary 328 BMWs. All were of 1,971cc. Common sense returned for the 'Big Six' 335 of 3485cc in a 1939–41 production span.

Some of the specially bodied 326s, or the later 327s – especially with the 80 horsepower option of the 328 engine (327/28) and a stunning variety of coachbuilt bodies in coupé or cabriolet style – were delightful to look at. They

Triple downdraught Solex carburettors dominate the engine compartment of this 328, still delivering lusty performance 55 years after departure from the factory gate

were almost as rare as the far better known BMW 328s, of which only 462 were made.

Those elegant thirties BMW bodies were repeatedly echoed amongst postwar designs, indeed the last original (badged as EMW) came from the communist-controlled Eisenach works in 1955. As a consistent class winner and founder of the all-BMW sporting tradition, the 315/1 also has a strong case for the BMW aficionado's respect.

However it is the 328 that has held the enthusiasts' imagination. Judging from contemporary film (thank you, both BMW and what was AFN at Isleworth, West London), it had a balance between all its dynamic qualities – particularly power and chassis – that made driving the 328 delight. The tubular steel chassis was at the heart of its handling quality, allowing outstanding strength to weight ratios to be achieved with comparatively soft suspension of the live rear axle and transverse sprung wishbone front layout. The complete two seater 328 weighed just 830 kg/1826 lb. That meant it had an unmatched power to weight ratio, as well as outstanding handling poise, amongst contemporary 2-litres.

The 328 version of that 1,971cc bottom half was topped by triple carburettor induction and unique valve gear. Operated via the usual single block mounted camshaft to directly prod the inlet valves, it utilised transverse pushrods to preserve the harmony of the classic hemispherical head design.

Born before the Second World War, but still the star of the show in the nineties, the Richard Martorell 328 at the 1992 BMW Car Club Dreher Park Concours, West Palm Beach. Richard has a wide range of cars – including the XK Jaguar that was inspired by the 328's lines after WWII – but he remains a fanatical follower of BMW 328 lore, tracking down many of the genuine survivors amongst the 462 recorded production examples. He says, 'my 328 has period performance modifications, including the Schleicher high performance cylinder heads, deep pan sump and ducted brakes. But the car does not run the 501 wheels that many others have photographed'. Richard purchased this 328 in 1982 and knows that it has lived in the Berlin of the fifties, Detroit and California

True, the head appears uncomfortably tall, but the central plug location for premium combustion at a further elevated 7.5:1 was assured and downdraught carburettors (Solex 30 JF, ex-factory) contributed to the outstanding production output of 40.5 bhp a litre, nearly twice that of the original single carburettor 320. In comparison, the 1992 BMW M3 straight six yields 95.6 bhp a litre.

Developing 80 bhp and capable of exceeding 93 mph in standard trim, the 328 was repeatedly tuned to yield more power. Co-designer Fritz Fiedler spent the immediate postwar years in Britain as part of the Bristol company's interpretation of war reparations. A 2.2 litre version of the Bristol-BMW was rated at 125 bhp for normal public road use before Bristol abandoned the six cylinder concept for American V8 horsepower.

Nemesis – the War Years

For some purists, we have now come to the end of the classic BMW car era. The Second World War brought BMW to an artificially high level of manpower (some of it from prison and concentration camps) and military output. BMW became a prime target for bombing of the most intensive 'round the clock' type. For BMW was not only an effective piston engine maker and a useful source of military transport. From 1939 onward it had been at the leading edge of developing axial flow turbojets (the 003 family), as well as pure rocket motors (P3390, and many more), which also had an application for the first Messerschmitt 163 jet plane.

The tiny Heinkel 162 'People's Fighter' (Volksjager) incorporated a single BMW 003E-1. A BMW that could deliver over 2,000 lb of thrust; enough to allow the tiny (29 ft long, 23 ft span) HE162 an astounding 1944 maximum of 562 mph at some 20,000 feet.

Such aviation work brought revenge upon not just BMW, but the city of Munich as well. Older residents still vividly recall how the sky would darken as the big daylight USAAF raids became commonplace whilst the nights became a literal fiery hell on earth, courtesy of the RAF. Company history records the arrival of up to 11,939 bombs weighing 1,839 tons during one 24 hour period (11 July 1944) at one site.

By April 1945 the Americans were occupying Munich. Worse still for the company hopes of any postwar production presence in the car business, their assembly and manufacturing base at Eisenach was firmly in the Russian sector. It would henceforth be infamous for the two-stroke rebirth of the Wartburg badge. Some 16 nations were reckoned to have shared in spoils that also included the BMW aero engine facilities at Berlin-Spandau.

The postwar path to ruin

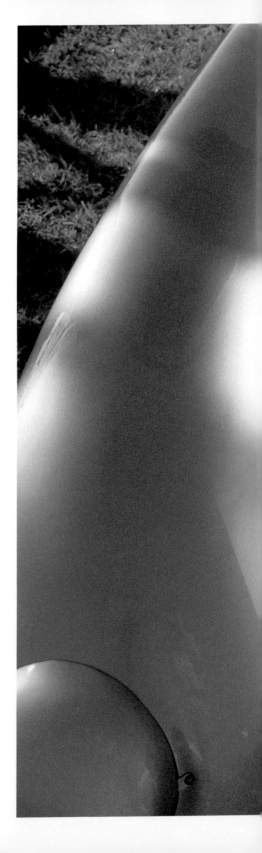

Returning to the car business postwar was not just hard for BMW, it was damn near impossible. The initial step from saucepans to motorcycle fabrication was not easy (R24 Boxer twin bike production was achieved by 1948). Just mentioning to the Allies the possibility of getting back into aero engine manufacture would have been enough to bring further constrictions on the painful rehabilitation of Bavaria's proud engineers in the initial postwar period. It was ten years after the war that BMW were granted a licence to rebuild their Allach aero engine facility, making the General Electric turbine under licence for the notorious Lockheed Starfighter.

BMW was the last of the German national car producers to make their comeback. Thanks to the British, even Hitler's Volkswagen vision was being manufactured in 1945, but it would be fully seven years (November 1952) before BMW could deliver their first postwar production car, the 501. And then, as was seen at its Berlin Show preview of 1951, it would have the prewar 1,971cc six of 65 bhp. It was 1955 before BMW had the freedom and finance to make their own bodies again, these initially constructed by later BMW cabriolet/M1 associates, Baur in Stuttgart.

German sources criticised BMW for putting such a 'weak' old motor into a fat (1,340kg/2,948 lb) four door, commenting that the lines were inspired by Austin in England. The loyal BMW public still bought 5,692 models between 1952 (when less than 50 were delivered after that protracted start) and 1955. By that time the 501 and its six cylinder cousins such as the 501A (now 72 bhp) had been joined by a 502 derivative of the large saloon that was unique.

The Slow Seeds of Recovery

Germany's first postwar production V8 of 90 degrees cylinder bank angle was an all aluminium design that was first offered at 2,580cc (74 mm × 75 mm) and 90 bhp, progressing to 3,168cc (82 mm × 75 mm) in 1956 for the 140 bhp Graf

Whilst BMW themselves struggled to return to car manufacture in the immediate postwar years, others such as Ernst Loof assembled amazingly sophisticated sports racers around 328 hardware. One of the best was the car Loof created before returning to work for BMW in the fifties: a 1949 Veritas-BMW Rennsport spyder with a winning history. It is owned by Florida's Gerry Sutterfield, who also owned a Veritas coupé in the eighties

Goertz rarity, coupé or cabriolet 503. Just over 400 of these handsome beasts were built between May 1956 and May 1959, but that looked like the peak of mass production beside the 150 bhp 507. This was a further 1956–59 step towards the exclusive high price niche, offered only as a two seater and with a reported run of just 252 copies. One of the most famous 507 owners is unique former World Champion John Surtees, who earned his titles on two wheels as well as four.

These V8 502 saloons and their mechanically similar 503/507 sporting cousins stopped the German press whining about weak engines and British cloned coachwork, but they did absolutely nothing for the BMW balance sheet. That was soothed a little by the bizarre contrast of the Iso Isetta licensed manufacturing deal for the narrow (rear) track four wheelers which used BMW single cylinder motorcycle power sources. These were numerically successful in 245 and 298cc guises (over 161, 360 made).

Above
The 501/502 series of 'Baroque Angel' saloons carried BMW back into car manufacturing in some style. This is the factory owned 502 V8 in Munich

Right
Imposing: BMW Vintage Club of North America representative at the 1992 West Palm Beach meet was this stately 502 V8. It could use a little cosmetic surgery, but was a welcome reminder of the company's postwar comeback period

Right
It does rain in Florida, heavily and suddenly. The static 502 V8 displays large rear window and ...

Above
... a gorgeous V8 badge, the first in postwar Germany

Isetta-BMWs were well known in markets such as Britain, where their single front doors and 53 mph/50 mpg capabilities were generically labled as typical of the 'Bubble Car' class, alongside Messerschmitt. The Isetta adventure eventually led BMW into a commercially useful avenue of light car production with the 600 (Boxer twin of 600cc/19.5 bhp) that had the longest recorded 0–62 mph claim the author has seen: 58 seconds! This was hardly surprising since the pioneer of trailing arm back suspension for BMW was only capable of 64 mph. Over 35,000 were made between 1957 and 1959.

Aside from the low production volumes achieved by the Goertz 503 and 507 exotics, the big six cylinder and V8 501/502 lines were hardly volume numbers: including every V8 derivative, some expiring in the early sixties, the grand total was 23, 120 vehicles. Only the 502-2.6 litre V8 saloon achieved truly volume production, exceeding 2,000 units a year in 1954 and the following year.

Better known classic BMW V8s were assembled by the hundred, or the handful: the 507 never exceeded 100 units a year. Some twists to the V8 theme such as the 505 state limousine – built for West German Chancellor Dr Konrad Adenauer – achieved a run of just two prototypes.

Above

The Graf Goertz lines of the 507 in the factory brochure seemed like something from the jet age in the fifties. From November 1956 to March 1959 hand built production yielded only 252 examples, with less than 100 known to exist in the late seventies. The best known example in Britain belongs to World Motorcycle and car Champion John Surtees. The only man to win two and four wheeler World titles bought his 507 new in 1957, used it regularly over large trans-European mileages until 1963 and has kept the car – plus a supercharged BMW motorcycle – to date

Right

'Go on, take a ride Hans'. A factory 503 is left out in the sunshine to tempt the Munich populace by an artful photographer

Motorcycle output kept the leaky BMW car production ship afloat though the mid fifties, but volumes declined as the German economic miracle raised consumer aspirations beyond two wheels. BMW recorded operating losses in all but five financial years between 1946 and 1960. It could not go on.

The crunch came in 1958 and was averted by using 6.5 million Dm of the reserves to soften a 12 million Dm loss. The balance was transferred to the 1959 balance sheets, when they made another 9.2 million Dm loss and had to dig into half the issued share capital. Whilst BMW management hunted with increasing desperation during 1959 for the finance to build a new product that would save them, a stop gap saloon and coupé range, built on the 600 format, staunched disastrous cash losses.

Dubbed 700 and crisply styled by Michelotti, it brought the Boxer twin format to more than 181, 000 owners from 1959–65. Its tough flat twin engine of 697cc (78 mm × 73mm) and 30–40 bhp grew into its car production role with such conviction that it powered both 2-door coupé and saloon bodies up to 84 mph and returned nearly 40 mpg. Those snail-like 0–62 mph times of the 600 were halved; the 700 was up to six seconds faster than the contemporary 850 Mini. At 20 seconds for the 700 Sport to complete 0–62 mph, there was a hint of competition success to come. The 700 coupé proved an extremely effective class winner with 56–75 bhp extracted from its plucky little air cooled cylinders in race and rally guise.

Significantly, the 700 further developed the trailing arm rear suspension that has been so much a part of BMW's attachment to the front engine, rear drive, layout. Instead of a single box section arm, the 700 attached to the body at two triangulated points, was angled on a near diagonal, and operated a long strut damper coaxial coil spring layout.

Rescue: Enter the Quandts

December 9 1959 marked the crucial board meeting at which the Chairman of the powerful Deutsche Bank issued a financial plan that amounted to a takeover from Daimler Benz. BMW's smaller shareholders – many of them BMW dealers with their livelihoods at stake – fought back.

Under the leadership of Frankfurt lawyer and accountant Dr. Friederich Mathern the minority shareholders were supported by a loan of 30 million Dm from the Allach aero business and determined to find another 30 million Dm from further outside sources. As BMW limped into the sixties the most significant stake in its financial future was taken by brothers Herbert and Harald Quandt; they acquired 15 per cent, mainly though taking the stock of a Bremen timber magnate, one who had inadvertently financed some of the BMW stop gap engineering in the late fifties.

Herbert Quandt, like so many BMW senior personnel, proved a long-lived (he died in 1982) and fiercely loyal personality. His financial influence calmed the banks and allowed BMW to begin planning the haul back to the immense prosperity that culminated in the multinational organisation that is flowering in the early nineties.

By 1993 Herbert Quandt was a memory and his third wife, Johanna, plus six children sired by Herbert, held the controlling interest in BMW. It is a family fortune estimated in billions of dollars ($3.5 billion in 1989). Estimates of the controlling Quandt shareholding in BMW varied from source to source.

The 507 was never produced in large numbers. This 1958 example was built in the eye of a financial storm

As BMW prepared to establish their manufacturing plant at Greenville-Spartenburg, South Carolina, USA, in late 1992, German financial personnel told me: "approximately 60 per cent is held directly in the BMW Ag by the Quandts. Around 1 per cent is held in association with other major BMW corporate investors, insurance companies and banks, in a separate holding company: Gesellschaft Fur Automobilwerte, usually dubbed GFA".

Not everyone in 1992 Munich writhed in corporate ecstasy. BMW could boast of 75,507 employees worldwide – there were under 1,000 in 1946 – but that hid the fact that Munich had removed 3000 jobs quietly in the summer of 1992. For BMW had just the same problems as everyone else in selling big, expensive, cars in the nineties. Particularly the V12s from an aging 7-series and the largely unloved 850i coupés.

In late 1992 it was possible to see that BMW had the strongest of hands in the independent car building business. In the midst of a fierce worldwide recession sales numbers were holding up well. The arrival of the 1990 3-series was particularly apt; it pushed sales in the American market up 30 per cent in the first half of 1992, when most other brands were desperately discounting their way out of trouble. At home it seemed certain that BMW would outstrip Mercedes car production for the first time in living memory, and they did, a 1992 record total of more than 588,000 BMWs made.

Now let us look at some of the classics that contributed to a U-turn away from bankruptcy and allowed 30 years of richly rewarding progress.

Over 23, 000 BMW 700 coupés were made and this in one of the few to survive in competition form within the USA

Revival

This is the point at which the BMW story starts to take on the current 'Ring of Confidence', one engendered by that vital product to appeal to the burgeoning West German middle classes. The restructured company could see the 700 generating enough cash to prevent BMW slipping into trading losses again, whilst swiftly designing their longer term saviour.

Luckily the aggressive body and engine design forces within BMW overruled the original four cylinder intention of a rather anaemic 1.3 litre. The 1.5 litre Neue Klasse four-door saloons emerged (somewhat shakily—there were a lot of teething troubles) from the Munich production lines in 1962.

The primary technical principles within the 177.2 inch-long saloon were to prove as long lived as BMW personnel, and as versatile. The four cylinder engine, with chain driven single overhead camshaft, hemispherical combustion chambers within the aluminium head (running 8.8:1 production compression in place of the prototype 8.2:1) was extremely tough, being built around a five bearing crankshaft in steel.

In the 1,500 application the engine served in an upright stance – a posture it was to repeat in its more powerful Motorsport applications – but by far the majority of its 3. 5 million production descendants (from 1.6 to 2-litres) were installed with an eye to a low bonnet line: one featuring an engine canted 30 degree slant to the right.

Such four cylinders were overhauled at regular intervals to cope with new octane ratings and unleaded fuel requirements in a more emissions-conscious age. They traced their lineage from 1962 to 1988, when the 1.6 litre M40 family (with belt driven overhead camshaft and subsequent 1.8 litre derivative) terminated its glorious reign.

It is also worth recalling that these extraordinary four cylinders served the contemporary 5-series, and it was that middle class four door which actually

Above

BMW and Glas were brief manufacturing bedmates in the sixties. Here is the result of that union, showing its best (rear three-quarter) aspect. The front is rather unhappy, with BMW corporate features grafted onto the Glas face. The pretty BMW (Glas) 1600 GT runs well and belongs to L&C Tunbridge Wells and was imported from South Africa in 1989. For BMW, the most positive result was the acquisition of the Dingolfing site, which is now a versatile production source and was vital in the return of the six cylinders

Left

Tranquillity beside a Florida fountain for a modern rarity: a 2000 that lived into the nineties. Note the replacement steering wheel and sun roof surround

Above

This superb 2002 automatic illustrates a purity of line that many regard as the expression of BMW ideals, particularly in America. This 1972 round tail lamp 02 has covered but 56,000 miles in twenty years

Right

The carburated 100 bhp BMW 2-litre combined pulling power and economy so ably that it was used in 2-door coupés, 4-door saloons and the first 5-series. This one is healthily engaged in motivating a pristine British 2002 Baur cabriolet

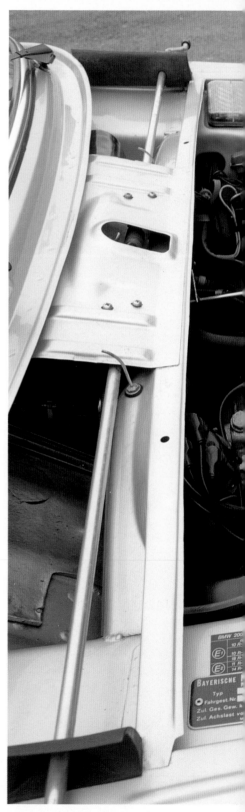

replaced the 1962–73 Neue Klasse, rather than '02' line. The latter served as both an introduction to adult BMW motoring and a sporting saloon of slight coupé pretensions.

Coded M10 within the factory, the four was deliberately designed to stand extra loads, especially a planned expansion to 1.8, and then 2-litres. In fact the iron cylinder block, carefully aged in the open air and strategically reinforced, not only served production engines up to 170 turbocharged bhp, but also encased 1.5 litre BMW Grand Prix turbo motors with outputs beyond the 1,200 bhp that could be measured by BMW Motorsport's dynamometer.

Therefore, it was significant that designer Alex von Falkenhausen had fought so hard – to the point of accusations of excessive temperament from his contemporaries – for such an 'stretchable' motor. One based on an iron foundation rather than the more fashionable (and equally temperamental at this time) aluminium alternative.

Other long lasting 1500 technical features included worm and roller steering (a basic ZF-Gemmer layout that lasted up to the 1975 3-series) and all independent suspension. This at a time when the live axle, or the rear engine car, ruled mass production formats. BMW utilised that European Ford favourite, the MacPherson strut front suspension, and a further update of the 600/700 trailing arm rear.

The 1500 also debuted a front disc, rear drum, braking system as a regular BMW feature – the 700 had all drums – the V8 saloons only listed discs as a 1959 option. So far as four cylinder BMWs were concerned, hard drivers had to wait for the advent of ABS braking to gain 4-wheel discs, but the 1977 BMW 323i of six cylinders did have a quartet of discs as a standard feature of the smallest BMWs.

BMW were under considerable pressure to get the 1500 into customer hands, for it had been debuted at the Autumn 1961 Frankfurt Motor Show and collected a lot of advance orders. These had to be fulfilled within six months – or face a fine from the organisers of the show. A small pre-production run met that show requirement, but the 1500s exhibited alarming fragility (especially of the gearbox and rear axle) initially.

Innovative American importer, Max Hoffman, was desperate for new products more suitable for the vast American market. BMW desperately needed the cash from such exports, but it was not until October of 1962

Above
The 02 face that scaled new heights of popularity for BMW in the USA

Opposite
Splashdown: Victor Koch of Georgia, USA, hoses down his stunning 1976 2002 in preparation for the October 1992 BMW CCA Dreher Park Concours. Victor reported, 'I bought it two years and 21,000 miles ago in a pretty sad condition. The paint was done in a car park, whenever we could get at it before the bugs got to it!'

(almost exactly a year after its Show debut) that volume production begun. Total output for 1962 was just 1,737 units. The 1500, for all its technical significance in establishing the ground rules of BMW middle class marketing, only had one big production year: in 1963 they made nearly 20,000 and the 1962–64 abbreviated span totalled just 23,557.

Throroughbred TI's

More significant to our sketch of BMW's rebirth was the logical bigger bore and stroke development of that 1,500 theme into the far more popular 1800/1800 TI (Tourismo Internationale) four doors of 90 to 100 bhp. Over 92,000 of the basic 1800s were made between September 1963 and August 1968, to speed cashflow out of the critical zone and toward prosperity.

The 1800s formed the basis of a fine motorsport racing and rallying saloon to refound the BMW sporting legend. Especially in the production of just 567 of the 130 bhp TI/SA (for Sonderausfuhrung; literally a special equipment special, sold only to competitors). On the way to the circuit, the 1800 TI/SA provided 116 mph autobahn pace, 0–62 mph in nine seconds and 17.7 mpg.

The 1800 TI breed put BMW back into competition contention with important commercial rivals such as Mercedes, Alfa Romeo and Ford. The 1800 TI proved that any frailties exhibited by the 1500 were a memory, regularly (1964–66) annexing its class, or overall victory, in the Belgian Spa 24 hour race, 'the Le Mans of saloons'. The company have continued to dominate the Belgian

event into the nineties, and look determined to continue doing so.

You could even see the 1800 TI/SA in replica (£55, 000 end of season sale price!) form racing the FIA Historic European Championship during the early nineties. Such a three car team was supported under the Scuderi Bavari label by a multi million pound BMW budget: they now care that much about their history at Munich. These four cylinder BMWs now humble the American V8s and English Ford Lotus Cortinas that could beat BMW in the sixties.

The sixties positive cashflow process was furthered by the advent of the slightly restyled (rectangular head lamps) 2000 four door. Almost 140,000 of all derivatives were made from January 1966 to January 1972. This includes the first (1969) batches (less than 1,000 in total) shipped for the USA. The 2000 capacity – based on a bigger bore for that tough iron block – was not fresh when it appeared in the saloon, since it had been debuted in a new BMW coupé, 2000 C/CS but more of that later.

Chronologically it was the 1500, 1600, 1800 and 2000 derivatives of that four-door Neue Klasse that put the lower spine back into a BMW recovery through the sixties, building on the stiffened resolve that had been generated by the acceptance of the BMW 700. The process would be completed by the rebirth of six cylinder car engine production.

Altogether 350,729 of the 1500 to 2000TI models were built. Put simply, they made it possible for BMW to expand beyond their Munich base and become such a confident company in the nineties.

In that expansive connection we should note that the company sold out of the aviation business in name at least, for some much needed cash. Ironically,

Left

Emerging from the gloom, just like the company, the 1800 (here Tourismo Internationale) was the enevitable development from the 1500. The 1500 to 200TI range was the bedrock upon which the BMW strength of the nineties was built

Above
At home in America: the 2002 became a Munich best seller thanks to enormous American demand. Fittingly, this one was found at Sebring by the Korman transporter. Ray Korman is one of the most vigorous competitive and commercial supporters of the North American BMW cause. Aside from regular competition, Korman Autoworks Inc, in the heart of NASCAR racing preparation territory (Greensboro, North Carolina) also engineered a series of turbo conversions for the marque, stretching from 3-series to V12 in 1992

Right
The Kugelfischer fuel injection 2002 tii developed 130 DIN bhp in standard European trim, and 125 SAE bhp for the USA, allowing over 115 mph in either case

BMW's name is still very much in the aviation power business today. BMW's aerospace interest is a pan European joint venture with occasional adversaries Rolls-Royce.

The expansion years

The sudden revival in car manufacturing fortunes created immense pressures to find more factory space outside the confines of Munich. The BMW the workforce would expand from under 7,000 in 1960 to 22,900 within a decade.

Such was the rate of expansion that BMW's 50th anniversary went almost unnoticed in 1966, beside the news that they had acquired the debt-ridden assets and the lower Bavarian Dingolfing base of Glas, also on the river Isar. Dingolfing is about an hour's drive north of Munich on traffic-clogged two-way roads that wind through flat agricultural land. I visited it in the mid-eighties to see 6-series coupé manufacture and it was obviously an exceptionally flexible facility, and has since made all sizes of post-1973 BMW.

As with the earlier departure of Borgward from middle class car manufacturing, the failure of Glas gave BMW an unopposed opportunity to advance. Glas failed to make the transition from the hugely successful Goggomobile 'bubble' car to profitable sales of their 1700 coupé (the first belt driven ohc engine seen in production) and its bigger V8 cousin (nicknamed 'Glaserati').

Initially Munich carried on making the Glas coupé at Dingolfing – even engineering its own 1.6 sohc unit and trailing arm rear suspension – but that lasted only for 1967–68 and 1,259 examples. By then it was apparent to BMW that the importance of Dingolfing lay in providing production facilities for a more diversified range. It is also relevant to note that the company moved motorcycle production to an old armaments site (Spandau) in Berlin during 1967.

By 1973, the single wooden factory of Glas was replaced by a pair of modern production line halls. Dingolfing has been home to 3, 5, 6, and 7-series production during the past 20 years.

The four cylinder engine, canted at 30 degrees for the 1800 and all four/six cylinder descendants to date, remained at the heart of statistical BMW progress. Especially in the succeeding 'O2' series of 1966–1977.

Stand and stare in wonder: stock 2002 carburettor motor (owner: Victor Koch) of 1976 and the same year, but Alpina modified 2002 twin carburettor (owner: Frank Miller) at West Palm Beach in 1992

BMW bedrock – the '02' series

Initially debuted at the March 1966 Geneva Show as the 1600-2, the designation was meant to show this was a two-door car at a time when BMW's staple product was the four-door Neue Klasse. As for the slant four engines, much of the '02' running gear was familiar from the bigger four doors, revised to work in a smaller and lighter body, one that was also marketed as a 2 + 2 coupé.

The basic '02' ingredients comprise an all independent suspension based upon MacPherson front struts and rear trailing arms, ZF-Gemmer worm and roller steering and a disc (front), drum rear braking system, servo-assisted from September 1968 on all models.

Gearboxes were initially four speed units, but Munich listed five speeds as options that really were available surprisingly early. This remark applied with force to the comparatively unpopular 1971-74 Tourings (a three-door small estate car design that prophesied the much more successful second generation 3-series Touring). The Touring was listed with a 5-speed that lucky classic collectors may also find has been optionally or retro-fitted to the 2002 Ti or Tii saloons. Next to the cabriolets, the Tourings were rare BMW '02' bodies, a total of 50,000 made during April 1971–April 1974. Some derivatives (the last

Above
For 1974 model year BMW had to install the Federal bumpers, adding 9.5 inches to the overall length. The body received much heavyweight reinforcement, as can be judged from a 200 lb kerb weight gain. This federal 2002 from Florida was on concours parade in 1992

Above right
In the flesh, the 2002 turbo did not seem quite so fiendish. I drove this excellent example, with differing registration plates (it was VPJ 854S), at ten year intervals in the eighties and nineties, courtesy of L&C at Tunbridge Wells

Right
The dashboard design of the 2002 was plain and simple. This is the 56,400 mile old 2002 turbo panel of the L&C collection turbo. Completed with 150 mph speedometer and 8,000 rpm rev counter red lined at 6,400 revs

year of 1802, and the 2002 automatic) amounted to less than a thousand copies.

In its long production span, the '02' suffix was incorporated, most famous in the USA in the importer's inspired combination of the 2-litre (nee 2000) motor and the small (50 mm shorter than the contemporary four door in wheelbase, 320 mm less overall length) saloon. The logically labelled 2002 was received with hymns of praise on the American side of the Atlantic. The USA prolonged its life into that of the following 3-series.

A post fuel crisis economy model for Europe, the illogically badged '1502' model (1975–77), allowed BMW a range starter 11 years after the 1600-2's debut. In all, the '02' line racked up the thick end of almost a million sales (881,194 including all variants and production sources). BMW would never want for cash in this era, for the replacement 3-series sold in excess of a million copies each for the first two generations (1975–1990).

Again the iron block four was at the core of a variety of sizes for the '02s': it went from 1,573cc and 75 bhp to the now familiar 1,990cc which allowed up to 170 bhp in the unfamiliar (1672 were made, most in 1974) turbo trim.

The turbo 2002

History will record the 2002 as something of a turbocharging pioneer, the factory team (directed by engines engineering chief Alex von Falkenhausen) racing the 2002 with some 270 bhp in 1969. That non-intercooled KKK-blown unit was notoriously unreliable, but it helped BMW secure another European touring car title against the Porsche 911, and provided some amusement as it set faster laps than the 4.7 litre Ford Falcons achieved.

BMW produced seven prototypes of a roadgoing 2002 turbo in 1973 and put it fully into production for 1974–75. This, the first European turbocharged production car, was born at the wrong time as fuel costs – and availability – were badly affected in the wake of the 1973/74 Arab-Israeli war. The stripey 2002 with its notorious 'mirror writing' logo on the front spoiler was an unwelcome reminder of BMW aggression when the public priority was fuel saving, hence the limited production. However, as a driving experience the turbo 2002 was absolutely stunning , its uprated chassis and standard rear limited slip differential coping well with the 170 bhp.

Of course, the turbo model was the quickest (131 mph, 0-62 mph in eight seconds) of the four cylinder small BMWs produced prior to the 1985 M3, but other 2002 variants were fine performers too. In the late sixties, the abilities of the 2002 (circa 110 mph on its 100 bhp and some 10 seconds 0–60 mph) were balanced by excellent average fuel consumption (frequently exceeding 25 mpg) and the power sliding fun of the comfortably suspended chassis.

The subsequent performance development of twin carburettor (120 bhp TI, LHD only) and tii models (Kugelfischer mechanical fuel injection allowed a

Right
European production pioneer: the 170 bhp KKK turbocharged and Kugelfischer injected 2-litre 2002 turbo power house of 1973

Below right
Respected British 02 restoration and repair specialists Jaymic ran this colourful version of the 2002 turbo in national club racing events

Above
Roof panel and rear hood section in place, the smartest of 2002 Baur cabriolets was this member of the L&C collection. It was acquired in 1989 from a fastidious 'His and Hers' husband and wife pairing. They also contributed an equally seductive six cylinder coupé, a CSL without the wing kit

Right
Baur cabriolet allows us this inside view of the 02 cabin at rest

suave 130 bhp) was not achieved at the expense of fuel consumption in fuel injection format, or of driving fun. These performance 2002s were musts for the upwardly mobile enthusiast of the seventies.

Of the logically labelled 1602, 1802 and 2002 road car variants, the most popular individual model run was the 85 bhp original 1600-2/1602 with 172,941 manufactured. Yet the 2002 in basic single carburettor/100 bhp specification ran it close with 152,610 made in the 1968 to August 1973 European run of round tail lamp models. A further 43,704 were made to American specification between February 1968 and August 1973.

What were the '02' rarities, aside from the obvious 2002 turbo? The majority of 1602/2002-based cabriolet production – in association with Baur of Stuttgart – was measured in hundreds as can be judged from the January 1968 to December 1975 totals of just 4,199 examples. The one to value was probably the worst drive, because of a 'floppy' body, the Baur built 1968–71 convertible, one without the distinctive roll over hoop. This offered a preview

of the clean style the factory would finally achieve only in full convertible production with the second generation 3-series.

The new 3-Series

The 4-cylinder derivatives of the 3-series were originally important for introducing big car principles from the 1972 5-series to a smaller car. Comfort and quality was at a premium over sheer pace and brio in the 3-series, so BMW took that basic format of slant front engine, independent suspension and two-door body into a far more refined, better ventilated, safer product. The result was worthy and extremely profitable: 1.364 million of the first, E21-coded, 'Threes' were made, from 1975–1982.

Technically, BMW changed how the MacPherson strut, trailing arm, layout was configured, but the noteworthy change of operating principle over the '02' line was the adoption of rack and pinion steering. In addition, enough space was left in the engine bay to allow for a later inline six cylinder, badly needed since the fours could no longer keep up with the demand for the ever better equipped (and consequently heavier) 3-series. It took the sixes to restore the kind of power to weight ratio that had made the 2002 variants legends.

A classic collector amongst the original 3-series 'fours' could look at the complex convertibles (again by Baur) or the rugged 320i/4 as fun investments.

BMW overhauled the styling of the second 3-series (coded E30) so conservatively that – as with the VW Golf or many Mercedes – casual observers could not tell the newcomer from the original in 1982. The E30 product was much more worthy, feeling very solid and civilised indeed, and it proved exceedingly versatile. The model was not without its problems, the majority electrical (frequently associated with the unique Service Interval Indicator), but the BMW reputation for fine cars now spanned a tempting 'ladder of opportunity' as the 3, 5, 6, and 7-series.

Amongst 2. 22 million examples of the later E30 theme there was the choice of doors in any combination from 2 (convertible, M3, saloon) through 4 (saloon) and 5 (Touring) and diesel engines from under 100 bhp to petrol units of 220 bhp. A 4 × 4 option was offered in saloon or touring body, suffix 'X' (as in 325iX).

Leaving aside the obvious M3 choice for collectors, I would say that the 3-series convertible (not replaced by the current E36 3-series equivalent until 1993) would be a worthy selection. All seem agreed that the lines, hood folded, are uncluttered and attractive and there was a wide choice of four, or six, cylinder power plants. The manual hood was a dream to operate and folded smoothly via a complex ball bearing mechanism, hiding beneath a neat panel.

A 3-series convertible will never qualify as a rarity (over 101,000 were made from 1985–1992), unless you select an M-branded Motorsport 'designer'

edition. Or the truly exotic M3 variant, of which fewer than 1,000 were made, many at BMW Motorsport itself, before the M5's late eighties success demanded Garching production space.

Time to look back to the six cylinder era that was born on the back of so much four cylinder success.

More deceptive 02 power. This 'M2' conversion implanted M3 power in an otherwise innocent 1976 model. Owner Tommy Charles from Alabama reported that one of biggest tasks was sorting out a suitable replacement computer management system for the ex-M3 unit in non-factory carburettor guise

Establishment

In 1968, less than ten years after facing either no future or life as a subsidiary of Daimler Benz, BMW had bounced back. Now they were confident enough to take on the Mercedes-Benz marque in the luxury saloon car market. Remarkable as that was, the car itself – a distinct stretch of all BMW principles, right down to the slant six cylinder developed from the original tough four – was a true BMW alternative to the Mercedes. Until Unterturkheim's engineering legions had a chance to retaliate with the superb 1971 'S'-Klasse, BMW proved very effective competitors, making more than 217, 000 such 'Big Bimmers' from 1968–77.

From the classic or collector viewpoint, the four-door saloons have not received the attention they deserve. Such saloons have been overshadowed by the style and motorsport glamour of the equivalent (though initially very differently bodied) coupés.

The new six cylinder BMWs were not that large at announcement time, measuring some 185 inches in length by 68.9 inches wide. Following criticisms of interior comfort, particularly in the back seats, and to stay with the Mercedes/Jaguar elongated wheelbase pace, BMW stretched the original 2.692 m/106 inch wheelbase some 100 mm/3.93 inches. The same bonus four inches reflected in the overall length of L-suffix saloons sold from 1975 until the range's 1977 demise to make way for the 7-series.

The existence of BMW amongst the Mercedes classes demonstrated the emergence of a very different atmosphere at BMW. Whilst Quandt supervised every key move from a financially magisterial position, the public saw an increasing amount of ex-Opel and Auto Union employee, now the BMW sales director, Paul G. Hahnemann. It was this aggressive personality who shifted the final stocks of the old era 700s and V8 502 descendants after his arrival in 1961. It was Hahnemann who seemed happy to tread where Baroque Angels (the nickname for 501/502) had proved so ineffective: right on Mercedes toes.

The big BMWs

Hahnemann's sixties spirit was perfectly attuned to BMW's equally ambitious engineers, typified by chief Bernhard Osswald and engines engineering ace von Falkenhausen. BMW's time had come; the larger capacity sixes would seem a convincing argument for joining the highest echelons of the German prestige market.

Technically, von Falkenhausen was initially a little dismissive of the creativity he and his team had applied to the inline six: 'it's just a bigger four', he insisted when we spoke in the seventies. Later in that memorable conversation he

Six cylinder heritage: the 277 bhp M1 of 24-valves and dohc layout alongside the 80 bhp cam-in-block 328 and the 12-valve, sohc, CSL they nicknamed 'Batmobile'

allowed how proud he was of its 8,000 rpm competition abilities in later life. BMW have commercial reason to thank the thirties BMW sixes; the German public remembered these as the 'true BMWs' through the worst of their fifties mismanaged blunders.

Back in the seventies in his beautiful family house in Munich, von Falkenhausen, a quietly spoken aristocrat with design credits in military and motorcycle hardware before he rejoined BMW in the fifties, underplayed his role in the six cylinder conception. He never did credit himself with the unique triple hemispherical combustion chamber that gave the six its unique blend of comparatively economical power, or its extensively counterbalanced 7-bearing crankshaft pattern, which made smoothly attaining a 6,500 public road rpm such a pleasure.

The 'Big "Four" element in the six was mostly plainly seen in the 30 degree slant configuration and the use of the 89×80 mm bore and stroke. One that

gave us a later 3-litre family of big sixes (1990cc in a four). Initially the chain-driven single overhead camshaft unit was freely available in 150 bhp/2,494cc capacity (86 × 71.6 mm) as the 2500. Production commenced in August 1968 (January 1969 for the USA), but it was always a two model range with an 86 × 80 mm bore and stroke for a 2,788cc 'Big Brother' sold as the 2800; manufacture begun in April 1969 (June for the USA).

Built around the usual BMW front engine, rear drive, layout the 2500/2800 featured either a manual 4-speed gearbox, or a rather unsatisfactory ZF 3-speed automatic. It shows how effectively BMW had penetrated the Mercedes and Jaguar establishment in Britain that an Autocar survey of 1976 estimated that 'perhaps 40 per cent' were equipped with automatic transmission.

The bigger engined saloon brought a bonus of 20 bhp (totalling 170 horsepower at 6,000 rpm) and allowed a credible 124 mph maximum speed claim. Obviously later derivatives would be even faster (over 130 mph from 1971 onward), so it was appropriate that the big sixes became the first mass production BMWs to have a quartet of disc brakes as standard equipment.

The rest of the running gear was to the BMW convention of MacPherson struts fore and trailing arms rear, but the 2800 had the refinement of Boge self levelling at the rear. BMW overhauled the ZF-Gemmer worm and roller steering. In a bid to lighten steering action they ended up with an elbow-pumping four turns lock-to-lock. A similar fate befell all 3-series, bar the M3, in the first two generations, despite the adoption of a precise rack and pinion system.

Both models had immediate worldwide appeal to those seeking a change from the prestige car establishment, rightly putting a premium on driving pleasure rather than plush comforts. To the author's mind the interior could not possibly have been described as lacking in creature comforts, and it established BMW as absolutely the best in respect of providing instrument clarity via the simplest of black and white graphics behind a single viewing pane, all placed before a driving position that would also be widely imitated. A further neat instrument panel touch was that automatic transmissions displayed which selector position was selected, a feature that some European marques still (unsafely, in my view) neglect.

Still contemporary German sources seemed to feel that 'they offered less comfort and less attention to many details than the Stuttgart Marque', although they did admit 'the big BMWs offered an engine which revved like a turbine'. They certainly did: I drove these big saloons regularly in harsh European race reporting conditions and will long remember an average of well over 100 mph maintained between Calais and Marseilles by myself and Motor Sport/Motoring

The 'Big Sixes' of the sixties and seventies were suave running extensions of the four cylinder breed. This is the biggest of the CSL sixes, the 3,153cc unit rated at 206 bhp

News production director, Michael J. Tee, in a 3.0 Si. Nor will I forget the ready and rapid manner in which a Munich-loaned 2500 swept back from Salzburg in Austria to its homeland, even though our first task had been to locate the car beneath the spring snow! They may have looked staid, but those big BMWs could certainly travel with a verve and vigour that I do not recall from contemporary six cylinder Mercedes or Jaguars.

BMW obviously thought they had got the recipe substantially right. There were few changes, aside from the long wheelbase variant mentioned earlier, and three further variations on the inline six cylinder theme. Those engines remained carburated in initial 3-litre guise. They measured 2,985cc, achieved by an extra 3mm in the bore to utilise ex-2002/2000 dimensions. Now 180 bhp was claimed at the previous 6,000 rpmand improved torque at an highish (for a prestige saloon) 3,700 rpm. The 3-litre also marked the replacement of ZF automatic transmission by a Borg Warner, also a 3-speed.

Fuel injection

The carburated 3.0 S for saloons lasted much of the seventies (1971–77) in Europe, but was not the flagship in Britain. That honour was held until 1974 by the fuel injected model: 3.0Si. This had the same engine dimensions but with 200 bhp at 5,700 rpm in its initial form. It was also available during the same seventies span. The 2,985cc was the recipient of replacement fuel injection during its production life, transferring in September 1976 production from D-Jetronic to L-Jetronic. All American production was in L-Jetronic trim. Reported European horsepower dropped 5 bhp and torque a fractional amount, primarily because the L-Jetronic move was accompanied by a drop in compression to 9: 1.

The 3. 0 Si was an extremely rapid big saloon: Autocar reported a maximum of 131 mph, 0–60 mph in 7.3 seconds (similar to their test results for the 2002 turbo), but you paid with 17.4 Imperial mpg at the 97 octane fuel pumps. Very few remain in the UK, partially because of the rust that also afflicted contemporary BMW coupés a decade on from manufacture, but also because they were totally undervalued (rather like old Jaguar saloons). Most were whipped to a neglected Inner City death.

The long wheelbase models were notable in our history for a 3.3 litre variations on a six pot theme. Initially a carburated 89 × 88.4 mm for 3,295cc and badged 3.3 L (1974–76 in Europe), it grew into a Bosch L-Jetronic injection unit of 3,210cc (89 × 86 mm) and 195 bhp that was labelled 3.3 Li.

The final 3.3 Li twist had more torque than any other big BMW six of the period, 29. 2 mkg /211 lb ft, but this was not available until 4,200 rpm. Incidentally these big capacity 3.3s were not shared with the CS/CSL line, but doubtless be a suitable alternative mounting, if you simply cannot get an original

325i, 2,494 cc, 84x75 mm, Z1. Some customers were not satisfied with the 170 bhp, feeling that the machine handled so well it could have taken more. They may well have been right

Above
Welcome within; BMW Technik ensured that the Z1 bore corporate identity but the environment within was unlike any other factory specification. The Z1's modest dimensions and outstanding chassis manners meant it was still a pleasure to drive in RHD Britain, vague gearchange aside

Right
I like the Z1 better with the hood down and the doors up, but there is no denying it has a uniquely open air feeling with the doors down and the ex-325i engine singing. This example of the zippy breed is retained by L&C in England

unit at an affordable price.

If you agree with me that the 2500 to 3.3 Li lines are overlooked by collectors (and are often ridiculously cheap by comparison to the equivalent BMW coupés), have a look at these production pointers. The 2500 was the longest lived in Europe , made during the entire 1968–1977 duration, but would be quite a USA rarity, with just 380 shipped in the first (1969) year and 366 made in 1970. Production finished by July 1970 at 750 units to prevalent Federal specifications.

The American 2800 was not made in more than hundreds either, until it expired in November 1971. Even rarer, and a much better driving experience even in US form (176 SAE bhp at 5,600 rpm; 0–60 mph in 9.5 seconds, 120 mph maximum) was the 3.0Si to American specification, of which 296 were made between 1974–5, presumably because of the period success of the less plush

Bavaria 3-litre package for the USA.

In Europe the 3.0 Si remains desirable, but common. Unless, that is, you take the automatic option: BMW were obviously having troubles in 1971 and 1972 with this option. The company confess to having made just three. And if you've got the 1972 3. 0 Si-automatic , it's the only one reported manufactured that year! By 1973 the 3.0 Si-automatic was a volume item, as planned.

That concludes our tale of the original big BMW sixes, but it is worth reminding ourselves that a completely new breed of small six arrived in 1977 for the 320, 323i and 520. Initially coded M60, then M20, this single overhead camshaft unit was specifically designed to fit the 3-series engine bay and is most clearly differentiated from its bigger brethren by the belt driven overhead camshaft atop the traditional iron slant block and aluminium head configuration.

This engine family grew to maturity with fuel injection for the short stroke 2-litre (1,990cc, 80×66 mm) to serve 320i/6 and 520i. A 2.3 litre Big Brother (2,315cc, 80×76.8 mm) was reserved for the 323i (in two bodies). It then became the versatile 325i motor (2,494cc, 84×75 mm) that also saw 170 bhp duty in the 325iX and a certain collectors' classic, the Z1.

One of the greats

The latter was pure 2-seater sports car of very unusual construction. The child of the advanced 'think-tank' brains at BMW Technik, Z1 featured bolt on glassfibre panels over a galvanised steel chassis. The 170 bhp 325i engine and five speed gearbox was slotted in aft of the front axle line. It hitched up to a new 'central arm' multiple link rear, whose effective principles were transferred to the 1990 (E36) 3-series.

On the road, the Z1 was a BMW revelation. Frankly, the company had been lagging on the handling and roadholding fronts with their smallest products. Excepting the M3, the 3-series of the seventies and eighties was heavily criticised for its wayward tail end manners (the Swedish even suspended the sale of more powerful six cylinder 'threes'), but the Z1 showed what BMW could do.

The Z1 always seemed to go where it was pointed; wheel spin was such a rarity that many clamoured for more power than the standard 2.5 litre M20

The lineage of the M1, M5 and M635 CSi (M6 to many) 24-valve engine family was firmly rooted in the 1974–76 European and American saloon car racing programmes. Here the 3.5 litre 1976 Daytona 24 hour-winning CSL of Brian Redman and Peter Gregg (actually it was 20.5 hours that year and ran from January into February). Seen as signwritten for use by Sam Posey and the expat Lancastrian at a 1992 promotion appearance for owners, BMW of North America

motor could yield. This despite a maximum reported at 136 mph with 0–60 mph in 7.9 seconds from *Autocar & Motor* in London.

The opportunity for more Z1 power came when this sohc small slant six evolved into current 24-valve, dohc, 325i/525i power unit (coded M50) of 192 bhp. But BMW were not playing power games with the Z1 and my insider rumours tell me that Z1 died because 'it was harder to sell toward the end of the run and because the space was needed for the later 3-series'.

The Z1 was full of ingenious little features – particularly the drop-down side panels, forming a unique open air motoring experience. It caused a small sensation when it was shown in 1986 and by 1988 the company had allowed it to go into restricted manufacture at the old Munich Pilot Plant (pre production) line. The anticipated volume was 5,000 units, reflecting the fact that this was not – despite its cheerfully compact appearance – a cheap sports car.

BMW made 8,000 of the Z1 by the official end of production in the Summer of 1990. It is quite possible that history will see this exercise as providing a 'halo effect' for whatever higher volume sports cars follow from the USA.

Family affair: one defined by owning some 30 examples of the BMW breed to date. British motor racing film and TV production demands have seen the Hay family from Worcestershire utilise just about every affordable BMW from their first 1602 to the six cylinder selection seen dozing alongside father Neville's white CSL. Wife Dorothy (Dot) is next to bespectacled Neville and drives BMWs too. Kiwi Sandy (next to husband Richard) and baby Abigail had the 50,000 mile 5-series in the background. Richard (right) had a lot of 3-series miles to his credit, including the E36 coupé on oversize rubber seen here. Also in the collection is the family 2002 touring and a CSi that is being restored around replacement panels (everything bar the roof) by CARS of Kidderminster. The chewed BMW steering wheel? The French bulldog, seen scuttling between Neville and Dot, terminated that £200 M Sport item!

Coupés

Specialities of the house (1937–1993)

Until the advent of the nineties 3-series coupés, I respected only the Wilhelm Hofmeister-penned BMW CS (Coupé Sport) in six cylinder guise as the inheritor of pre-war BMW virtuosity in the rakishly elegant art of building beautiful coupés.

Motoring history tells us that the 1937–1941 coachbuilt (mainly Ambi Budd) 327 and 327/28 were the foundations of this great tradition. Those 1971cc originals were part of a prewar BMW breed (326/327/328) that the German public still recognised as 'true BMWs' when the company commissioned Dr Bernt Spiegel to research its home customers in the sixties.

There was some recognition of postwar products as BMWs, particularly the 2 + 2 700 CS, which had an extraordinary impact considering only 27,181 were made compared to 119,449 of the saloon that followed it into 1959 production.

The obvious candidates for classic status, such as the V8 fifties and early sixties saloons and counterpart coupés/sports cars (503/507) were treated almost as aberrations. Like the Isetta they were 'not typical' of a 'proper' BMW according to the results of that early sixties research. This led directly to BMW's employment of the niche marketing policy that is now so desperately imitated around an automotive world hungry for profit beyond volume.

Coupés, whether from BMW or anyone else, are an emotive subject. You nearly always pay more for less (two doors instead of four, less passenger space and so on). Customers – myself included – still happily purchase these wheeled beauties on emotional grounds rather than any automotive logic. I know, I have bought from a brochure, without seeing more than superb studio photography of my 2 + 2 intended.

From the enormous selection of coupés provided by BMW history, I have used the emotional process to select what you see and read about in this section. It is the most personal section of the book and my personal BMW nominations for glorious transport and static beauty are as follows: the 327, the 3200 CS, the 3.0 CSi and the M635 CSi. The current 3-series coupés would also get my vote in 325i or M3 form, if only I could find the perfect combination between elegant appearance and driving dynamics.

The current 2-door outline is the epitome of elegance, but neither its 192 bhp engine or handling biased so heavily toward understeer belong on my list of

Early days: the sweeping two tone lines of the factory 327 coupé were available from October 1938. The 2-door was available with a standard 55 bhp (78 mph maximum) or the ex-328 motor of 80 bhp (designated as 327/28) with near 90 mph abilities

Left

*New nose in town: Wilhem Hofmeister penned the in-house lines of the 1965 2000
C/CS, which debuted the 2-litre stretch of the four cylinder 1500/1800 motor*

Above

*American generation trio: the original four cylinder 2000 CS (that is the 120 bhp
version, rather than the 100 bhp 2000C) snuggles up to a clean white 3. 0 CS. To
their left, the Power Plant of Burlington, North Carolina development of racing CSL
themes. In 1992 Power Plant offered a range of engine and transmission services
from a $2,000 2002/320 rebuild to a monstrous 6.1 litre/435 bhp stretch of the
750i/850i 5-litre V12 for $19,750*

Left
Most of the four cylinder Hofmeister 2000 coupé body made it over to the six cylinder era. We can see here that the tail lamps clusters were similar, but not identical in the ornamentation that surrounded them for the CS versions of 2000 and 3.0 coupés. The rear window 'dogleg' and badge also remained, the classic rear window outline a feature of all current production.

Above
I thought this was one of the nicest coupés around town for the USA Oktoberfest, as well as one of the furthest travelled. It had ventured over a thousand miles down the Eastern seaboard from its BMW Car Club of America Massachusetts base

Automotive exemplars. The new M3 six belongs with the wheeled Gods, but the handling is flawed by a lack of wet weather consistency and is also aesthetically spoiled for me by the front aerodynamic 'shovel'. It needs balancing by a rear appendage, or a chunkier overall body style to compliment its purpose.

Dreams and lost opportunities

First of these personal favourites: the 327. I admit it, the separate chassis Eisenach machine is a total dream in coupé form. Just 179 were made (according to non-factory sources), whereas more than a thousand of an equally charming convertible were manufactured, but its rakish charm captivated me. However, I do not want to spoil the enchantment by driving its elegant outline, especially not at the maximum of 87 mph promised by the 327/28 transplant.

A 327 is desired on a sheer 'pin-up' attraction and – unlike the 328 – I would not expect much from the actual driving experience. In outline I think it is the perfect expression of thirties appeal, without the heavy handed echoes that my family's elderly (1927 and 1939) Rolls-Royces left on my young mind.

The 3200 CS is a personal regret, for my home town played host to one of these 1962–65 machines. Its Bertone of Turin body was frequently parked next to my transport in the early eighties. To my regret I could not raise the modest £5,000 or so that was asked on its disposal through the pages of *Motor Sport* magazine, for only 603 of these 3. 2 litre V8s were made and I rather liked its hint of coupé lines to come. And I might have enjoyed driving that alloy V8 in 160 bhp trim, although I must admit a 507 sports car (as demonstrated and hill climbed by Hans Stuck senior) would be likely to give more dynamic satisfaction, as it does to John Surtees. The 3.0 CSi? More personal sentiment I'm afraid, this time associated with deep sporting satisfaction. The 200 bhp CSi was the basis of the 'Showroom Class' Group 1 winner (7th overall) that I drove at the 1972 Spa-Francorchamps 24 hour race. I think the six cylinder CS/CSi family the epitome of civilised speed: aside from sore palms on the large standard steering wheel, the 100 mph plus average ride over public roads that comprised the 8 mile lap left partner Peter Hanson and myself with more than enough energy to lift a glass. Nothing went wrong mechanically, despite pressing its 3,000 lb/1,400 kg kerb weight to more than 130 mph on standard wheel bearings in those long Ardennes curves.

Classic form: the concours 3.0 CS of Amy Lester has received a lot of personal attention from its lady owner, who does much of the work around the car herself. The Atlanta, Georgia, resident has nothing to with the motor trade, but the car exceeds professional standards in its presentation

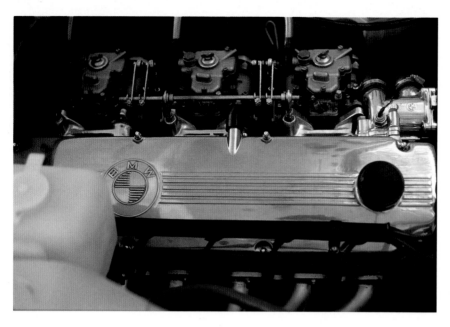

Above
*The engine of the Lester coupé remains carburated and of six cylinders, but otherwise
the rebuild that brought the triple Weber carburated unit to a reported 270 bhp
tackled pretty well every fundamental aspect, both inside and outside the Munich
straight six*

Right
*Unfortunately the dumb author left the passenger window down, but the elegant side
view of the six cylinder CS, appropriately plated 'MS-BMW', remains satisfying*

Champion car: the CSL

History's Automotive Hall of Fame will nominate the lightweight (CSL) variant
with its use of some unstressed alloy panels, as will most BMW fans. The
combination of an enduring motorsport legend and the potent image of the
racing 'Batmobile' with its wing set rampant, is unlikely to be eradicated. The
CSL dominated the European Touring Car Championship from 1973–80 and
raced with success from Le Mans to the American IMSA series.

Yet defining the CSL was always tricky as some early examples had Solex
carburated engines instead of the listed Bosch D-Jetronic; none could be
delivered to the German public without the aerodynamic kit stowed in the
boot. Furthermore the British order for 500 'CSLs' (manufactured September
1972 to January 1973) dispensed with the wing kit, and had far more luxury

items than the Germans had envisaged when paring it down from the 1,400 kg of the similar CSi, to an official 1,270 kg/2,794 lb.

Officially, the 1971-75 CSL had two Bosch injected variants on a six cylinder theme and an original 2,985cc carburated unit of 1971, shared with the contemporary 3.0 CS. For racing purposes a capacity beyond 3-litres had to be recognised, so a tiny overbore (89.25 mm instead of 89 mm) tolerance was included on the homologation papers to give an official 3,003cc from 1972–3. Power claims remained at 200 bhp of the contemporary 3.0 CSi. Finally the works wanted to race at 3.5 litres and a further capacity increase for the road cars was recognised: 3,153cc (89.25 × 84 mm) with a small performance boost. One of these was quantified as 206 bhp at 5,600 rpm.

Performance of these six cylinder CS coupés went from a claimed 125 mph (0–62 mph in 10.5 sec) for the 1974–75 fuel economy crisis 2.5 CS to 150 bhp and the 140 mph of a wing-kitted Batmobile on 206 bhp. Even a standard 3.0 CSi tested by Autocar in 1972 returned 7.5 sec for 0–60 mph and 139 mph.

Coupled to 20.7 mpg and 0–100 mph in 21 seconds, the CSL made road as well as competition sense. This was an aspect Motor Sport investigated in a tour of ten European capital in four days. They averaged up to 124.7 mph in some autoroute hours with a peak of 146 mph timed on a long Italian straight at 6,500 rpm in the standard top (four production gears only). Not surprisingly average consumption plummeted to 15.13 mpg, but their only operational complaint seemed to be the CSL fixed back bucket seat, which prevented sleep for the co-driver during this 3,789 mile 'Adequate Road Test'.

I know the original 2800 CS (1968–71) was flawed, and far too heavily based on the previous 'slant eyed' 2000 CS four cylinders for handling comfort. Later, as with the 3-litre coupés of 1971, BMW would ensure that more of the six cylinder saloon technology crept into the CS floorpan, which traced lineage back to the 2000 Neue Klasse.

I read the magazine reports on how the 2800 CS wriggled in corners because of its non-thoroughbred pedigree. I drove the original hard enough on the road to know that it was not the most rigid bodyshell constructed, but it was still a contemporary pleasure to conduct, with a civilised flair not available elsewhere. In fact, any of the six cylinder CS/CSi machines of that 1968–75 run were refined fun. I can see why the total production run amounted to 44,237 (including the rarer 2000 C/CS fours total of 13,691).

Collectors are inevitably going to plump for the CSL; the factory records I hold (issued 14.3.86) show a total of 1,096 made, 500 as indicated for Britain, and 539 for other markets (September 1972–June 1973). Finally (June 1974–November 1975) a batch of 57 is recorded as 3. 0 CSi L derivatives. I think this may have been the last batch of even lower weight racing shells.

'And so we say farewell to MS-BMW, most assuredly the cleanest coupé at Sebring'.

These served private and works supported teams after the CS/CSi officially became obsolescent in production terms. Nevertheless the CSL raced on into the era of the 6-series with apparently unstoppable success.

As with the transition from the '02' line to the 3-series, I initially found it hard to accept the almost angular 6-series coupe (1976–89) as substitute for the pillarless elegance of the CS.

I was wrong, commercially and competitively. BMW made more 'Sixes' than its predecessor and it went on to provide a fine competitor in the European Touring Car Championship. The 635 CSi won the 1986 title and Spa 24 hours before the M3 could be readied. Its sturdy endurance racing speed and modest 285 racing bhp were exploited by the likes of 1986 Mexican GP winner, Gerhard Berger. The Austrian then drove a Benetton-BMW, the last GP win for that BMW 1.5 litre turbo.

Unlike the CS series, I plump for the sportiest and fastest variant: M635 CSi. Although tipped for participation in European racing, the M635CSi was never made in sufficient numbers to qualify, with just 3,175 built in the first two full production years (1984/5) when the Group A racing requirement was for some 5,000 units annually.

The 6-series was conceived in a very different climate to that of the CS, and a major development pre-occupation for the engineers under the retiring Bernhard Osswald was to achieve American crash test standards (thus the loss

Off to the concours, classic BMW style. Courtesy of the Glarnes family, who have motored their Ontario, Canada, based CSL 'M-BMW' down to Florida. We are off to see some other CSLs . . .

Above
Classic coupé corner, American style. The CS/CSL contingent in the pine paddock at Moroso in the winter of 1992, some seriously shiny wheels to the fore

Right
The run of 500 British RHD specification CSLs spread far and wide in twenty years. Here is one of the official '3. 0 CSL' batch on concours duty in Florida

of that beautiful pillarless side glass). All this was to be achieved without boosting the weight unbearably beyond its predecessor, and the accompanying 7-series. Visually, French chief BMW stylist of the period – Paul Bracq (ex-Mercedes) – tied the 6 and 7 as tightly as the earlier saloon and CS had been but (again) appearances were deceptive.

For the 6-series rested on a 5-series saloon floorpan and as much of that lighter running gear as possible: not to save money, but weight. BMW were only moderately successful: by the advent of the 1981 635 CSi derivative (sohc-12v) BMW were up 120 kg/264 lb on the previous 3.0 CS and had only 18 bhp more (218 bhp at 5,200 rpm, 224 lb ft of torque by 4,000 rpm) to propel their 2-door.

Few were impressed by the price/performance ratios exhibited by the original 630 CS (184 bhp) and 633 CSi (200 bhp from the old 3210cc), a remark even truer in the USA. There, SAE emissions-strangled yields for the 633 wavered from 176 to 181 bhp with increased kerb weights (1,495-1,560kg) and depressed torque.

Another original 6-series problem highlighted by the Americans was that of quality control on body manufacture. BMW took the assembly chores away from Karmann at Osnabruck (August 1977) and left the now famous purveyors of convertibles (VW Golf, Escort) with only bare shell assembly and shipping to the assembly plant at Dingolfing.

The 635 variant was a necessity to maintain the sporting reputation of the big BMW coupé. It was timed beyond 140 mph , but was unable to match the earlier coupe in acceleration, resting on 8.5 seconds 0–60 mph. However, the 635 CSi would account for the largest CS/CSi production percentage from its June 1978 introduction.

The M635 CSi built on that 3.5 litre basis, actually a more reliable 3,430cc from June 1982. I had a unique opportunity to drive the 12-valve variant down to Munich to meet the then new M (for Motorsport) 24-valve bomber. This was certainly a contrast: I had thought the 635 CSi magnificent in its civilised pace (albeit a bit vague in crosswinds at speed, despite the added spoilers), but the M635 was in a different league.

The 24-valve engine bellowed mightily, yet smoothly, to 7,000 rpm. The uprated suspension allowed the most astonishingly manageable (and satisfying) rear drive handling I can recall. Modestly extended wheel arches and front spoiler gave just that flip to overall character that made the M-version a worthy inheritor of all that BMW breeding. Later, when I was alloted the chance of performance testing the 286 bhp M635 for Performance Car (showing an honest 150 mph and 0–60 mph in the six second bracket), I simply could not find track fault with the balance of the car. Like the factory team, I only wished there was an opportunity to race it.

Inside another RHD emigrant, this time a 3.0 CS. The original dashboard and wooden steering wheel has been lovingly preserved. This car was originally registered FNV 9L in the UK

The badging belongs to an original and fully equipped LHD road 'Batmobile', a rarity
at the time and set to become as significant as the 328 beyond the year 2000.
The 6-series coupé was not enthusiastically received in the USA (seen here at Sebring)
until more engine power was supplied. American feedback demanded that the
complete body was the responsibility of BMW rather than the subcontractor an
arrangement that covered early 6-series and all 2.0 to 3.2 litre C, CS, CSi, CSL
derivatives of its predecessor

Above

Moroso, Florida, October 1992. You needed 3.5 litres and an M6 badge to impress the largest export market in the World with the merits of the 6-series coupé

Left

More angular than its predecessor, the 6-series is still an impressive sight in clean condition

Mmmm: the concours judge ponders the M6 of NSA water treatment marketeer Steve Castle at Dreher Park, West Palm Beach. From Atlanta, Georgia, Steve had then owned the 1988 BMW for just over a year and it had 78,000 miles recorded. He recalled that, when bought, 'the paint was pretty desperate, especially at the front'

More on the M1 later, (see page 107) but here is the coupé from 1979. A complex gestation and a sorry production life, but a mid-engined performance machine to covet. Pride of place (left) at the BMW museum

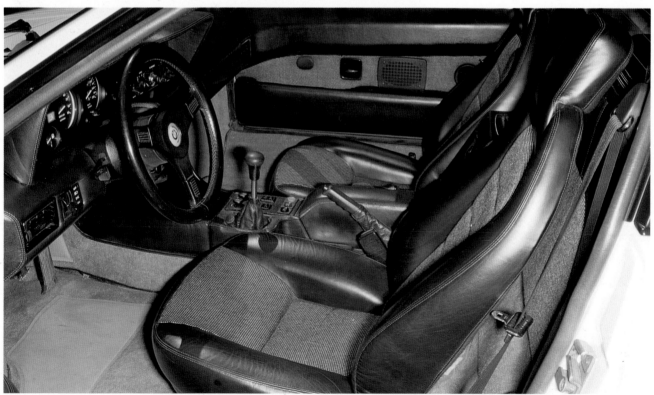

Above

The uncompromising face of the 6-series reigned for 14 years in Europe, from 1976 to 1990

Left

Is the M3 a classic? And if so, is it a true M-car or a worthy CSi replacement that should have been badged 330 CSi? Such questions occupied British motoring men in the 1992 winter: Autocar & Motor *staff photographer Stan Papior awaits a moody Majorcan sunset on its December debut*

Competition credentials

On June 16 1992, armed with a 3.8 litre/340 bhp BMW M5, I set out on a sentimental journey. Over a thousand miles across Britain, France and Belgium to Germany. There, I found the commercial result of BMW's oldest emotional involvement: competition.

I had worked at Ford Motorsport alongside Jochen Neerpasch and Martin Braungart, the men who formally founded BMW Motorsport GmbH in that surprise Ford-to-BMW defection of June 1972. Now I was to see the results of 20 years of endeavour, translated into an enormous Nürburgring celebration of 500 employees and their multi-million pound turnover.

In fact 1992 was a big year for BMW Motorsport. Beside racing the old M3 four cylinder for an undignified sixth season, the personnel on two Munich sites, Preussenstrasse (just behind the four cylinder tower) and Garching (the equivalent of an outer suburban trading estate site), were pushed mercilessly. They launched the new M3, an enlarged motor for the M5 (the last use of the classic 24v 'Big Six' of M1/M5/M635 CSi ancestry?) and an M5 Touring derivative. Add an increasing commitment to BMW Individual (mainly cosmetic trim and paint tailoring), and the fierce fight to make the inline six cylinder M3 racing car work, whatever the on/off plans to actually race would bring in 1993. You can see that Karl Heinz Kalbfell had plenty to direct in that 20th anniversary year.

In fact the history of BMW in motorsports goes back much further than 20 years. Even if we ignore the complicated antecedents of Wartburg and Dixi, have no doubt that the quickest of those white 328s at the Nürburgring (from June 1936 onward) were factory cars. The postwar period did dent availability of motorsport materials, but Alex von Falkenhausen raced to prominence with his own 328-based AFM (this 'M' for Munich) for Hans Stuck Senior, before rejoining the company in 1954.

BMW Motorsport

It was von Falkenhausen's restless spirit that truly founded today's BMW Motorsport GmbH, for he would rally or race the company products (from big V8s to the 600) with ruthless speed. It remained an informal process until the sixties. Then von Falkenhausen oversaw the hiring of formal competition managers whilst the 700, 1800 TI, 1800 TI/SA and 2000 TI became ever more effective touring car competitors.

By 1964 BMW could win outright in major endurance events such as the Spa 24 hours and have since remained the dominant force in European and national saloon car events. Of course they have been beaten, but for consistent

Immediately postwar, the Veritas racing streamliner from Ernst Loof showed individual interpretation of the way the 328 could shine in competition, for the factory were not permitted to make cars, never mind racing cars. Car, courtesy of Gerry Sutterfield, Florida

Above

Don Gibbs from Winston Salem has owned this ultra rare (especially in the USA) 700 coupé for 'about ten years. It has 25 coats of lacquer paint'. After all that effort, it seemed a shame that the car was likely to be sold soon after this picture was taken

Right

The immaculate engine bay of the Gibbs 700. The Boxer engine was rebuilt by BMW Fort Worth Texas and was thought to develop rather more than the factory used to enjoy in the sixties. 'Somewhere in the 68 to 70 bhp area, 'thought Don Gibbs some 30 years after the coupé had been privately campaigned in Europe and America

success in 'tin tops' the badge you need comes from BMW.

Over the years the 2002, the large CS/CSi and legendary CSL coupés (350 to over 800 racing horsepower), plus the later 3 (Group 5 and M3) and 6-series have all been winners. They reaped factory or factory-backed (in association with outfits such as Alpina, Schnitzer, Bigazzi and Prodrive) competition success. Even the 5-series won European and South African saloon racing honours.

Formula car victory, using their four cylinder iron block family under the M12 code, was tough to come by in 1967. BMW established themselves as championship winners in 1973 European Formula 2 and went on to secure six such titles by 1982. By then the 'motor men of Munich' under von Falkenhausen apprentice Paul Rosche were on course to secure the World's first Formula 1 Grand Prix title for a turbocharged car.

BMW achieved that, after another stormy start, with the 1983 Brabham team. The talents of Nelson Piquet in deploying their 640 bhp/11,000 rpm 1.5 litres were matched by designer-manager Gordon Murray. Today the BMW Motorsport/Paul Rosche/Gordon Murray alliance lives on in the provision of the 6-litre/580 bhp V12, created exclusively for the McLaren F1 road car developed under the management of Murray.

The dazzling record of victories created a natural demand for replicas. For example, over 500 of those M12 family Formula 2 engines were delivered at very profitable prices. These days BMW Motorsport can point to the delivery – by the hundred at dizzy prices – of complete M3 racing car packages, or any of the myriad components that make up a racing machine.

Back in the seventies Jochen Neerpasch had taken the fledgling Motorsport department into all sorts of areas to try to create post-Arab/Israeli fuel crisis funds. Today they no longer supply the fancy jackets and other items of apparel

Above
Neat little number: The Don Gibbs 700 coupé at Moroso Motorsports Park for the 1992 BMW CCA celebrations of BMW Motorsport's 20th Anniversary

Right
The way we were: compare this interior picture of the 700 cockpit with that of the Bastos 1992 M3 on page 123

Above
The 2002 was successfully campaigned in the prestigious American SCCA series, as well as the European touring car Championship. Here is one of two examples owned by Reg Cunningham being exercised at Sebring in that Trans Am trim

Left
The 700 racing coupé at rest in Moroso Motorsports Park; thought to be one of less than half a dozen running in the nineties USA

for public sale. Yet the Motorsport habit of providing contracted racing drivers with cars of interesting engine transplant or development units (such as a CS with a V12, or the more common big six transplant into 5-series beyond then factory standard levels of the 528i) bloomed into an increasingly commercial activity.

The M1 and the Procar series

The tidy historian will simply credit the mid-engined M1 as the first product from Motorsport GmbH. Although the M1 was important, its gestation was complicated. The evolution from a 1977–78 prototype, one that could not be made by Lamborghini, to the July 1978 to March 1981 manufacture run of 450 examples (49 for racing only), in association with Baur, was hardly that of a true 'in-house' product.

Above

Over 470 bhp from 3.5 litres was the job allotted to the CSL 24-valve unit that went on to become parent to the M1 road car unit, and thus to M5 and M6 motivation

Left

Forget the absent bonnet badge and Richard Conway's 1973 CSL makes the most photogenic of racing BMW coupés

The true path of what would come, with Motorsport inspiring a main company production line design, came in the form of the 1979-80 M535i. The first 5-series was equipped with the 218 bhp 12v six of 735i. This evolved – as did the production 5-series itself with a smoother version of the boxy body from 1981 – into a 535i M second generation and consequent 24-valve M5 of 1984.

That 286 bhp 3.5 litre provided a 150 mph four door. The engine had Motorsport history, being an electronically managed, slant rendition of the original upright (M88) M1 road car motor (then 277 bhp) unit. In fact the lineage goes back to the gear-driven camshafts of the racing powerplant that saw service in later CSLs.

Then there was the logical step into the 3.5 litre 24v version of the technically similar 6-series coupé (the M635 CSi–see previous chapter). This path can be traced to the nineties M5/M5 Touring, which uses a 3,795cc (90 × 94.6 mm) stretched version of that honourable 'Big Six'.

What happened to the M1? A rarity amongst mid-engine machines in

The 1973 Conway CSL is based at R. C. Motorsports in North Carolina and reportedly the car that the company used to win the Group 2 class within the 1973 Le Mans race, eleventh overall in the hands of Holland's Toine Hezemans (that year's European Champion) and BMW loyalist, Dieter Quester

Above

Fabulous achievement: just a small selection of the cars attracted by Richard Conway/BMW CCA and BMW of North America to support their 20th anniversary celebrations. Here the left to right scenario includes the number 5 Brabham BT52-BMW of the type raced to the 1983 World Formula I title by Brazilian Nelson Piquet, the Chevron B16-BMW raced by Dieter Quester in European historic events of 1992 and the many prototypes used in American events, including the 1986 GTP-BMW turbo closest to camera on the right

Left

Billed as the 'Fire and Wind' BMW, this McLaren 320i Turbo (one of three constructed and run from the Livonia McLaren premises between 1977-79) is the well preserved property of BMW North America. Regular driver David Hobbs remembered it in 1992 as 'a terrific car to drive, but it could have been even more successful than it was if BMW had been able to concentrate on this programme rather than the M1. At best it had 650 bhp, but it could have been 800, to judge by the 950 bhp BMW could get from much the same four cylinder turbo in the later GTP'

providing absolutely safe handling on the limit, as well as the expected 160 mph plus thrills, it was also artificially promoted into a one-marque racing series.

BMW Motorsport backed an enormously expensive Procar series of support races to selected Grand Prix that lasted for two years. This provided Brabham team mates Niki Lauda and Nelson Piquet with titles in the most expensive one marque series ever held until Tom Walkinshaw's Jaguar XJR-15 challenge of 1991. The M1 was most effectively raced against other marques in America; the Red Lobster team of 1981 dominated the IMSA/Camel GTO category with 12 wins and numerous lap records.

The M1 was an expensive blind alley in BMW Motorsport history, causing the main BMW board to look hard at what was going on. Jochen Neerpasch was out by the time production had finished and the company was reset on the eighties course that would bring them their own Formula 1 engine. BMW had been originally contracted to supplying the 1. 5 turbo to Talbot in France.

M3 and late eighties domination

As for Motorsport itself, the M5 and 6-series derivatives of the 24-valve engine were a preview to the much more popular 3-series machine that they engineered into 1985-1990 production on the main company lines at Munich: the M3.

Some 17,184 of the unique 4-cylinder, 16-valve, dohc machines would be made. A further 786 convertibles were made, some by Motorsport at Garching. Additionally, 330 racing M3 packages were supplied, so the M3 was numerically by far the most successful Motorsport product to date.

The M3 was created around a beautifully detailed front engine, rear drive, layout. Technically you could say all the usual BMW features – slant four cylinders, MacPherson front struts, trailing arm rear suspension – were present. Yet BMW worked on every aspect, especially the bluff body, to produce the basis of the most effective racing saloon. It had both a respectable aerodynamic drag factor and stability at racing speeds to over 170 mph.

For the public, M3 started at 200 bhp (195 with a catalytic convertor) and 2.3 litres, enough to allow over 140 mph and 0–60 mph in six seconds. A gradual evolutionary programme to support the racing programme, and 'limited edition' sales, allowed up to 220 bhp for the showroom and ever larger spoilers.

Finally, from winter 1989 to spring 1990, there was a 2.5 litre Sport Evolution. Some 600 examples were assembled in 1990 after a six month

The Nelson Piquet Championship Procar M1 now lives in the USA in the care of Oliver Kuttner. The powerful Procar still takes its exercise regularly, as seen at Sebring, 12 years after its European triumphs

Detail and an overall look at the most famous racing 635 CSi of all. This is one of the CSi coupés that conquered Europe and won the Spa 24 hour race, Schnitzer's BMW Original Teile machine, Teile meaning parts. An original that performed with fabulous reliability on its production base (peak power was only 285 or so, about that of the European M635 CSi street car!) against the wave of turbos from Ford and Volvo

development period: shades of the old BMW! The Sport Evolution gave 238 public road horsepower for a genuine 150 mph. In race trim the 2.3s were always credited with some 300 bhp, or more, but the M3 that won the 1987 Tour de Corse had a more flexible 285 bhp from Prodrive.

As the Germans relaxed their racing regulations over the six seasons of the M3's home competition life (it won the 1987 and 1989 German titles, plus two European and one World Championship amongst innumerable achievements), 9,000 rpm power flowered in the 2.3 and 2.5 litre fours. Certainly 370 bhp was possible , allowing BMW to stay reasonably competitive with the aerodynamically rather more radical Mercedes 190E 2.5/16 Evo II, once the M3 had received a 40 mm spoiler set extension.

The four cylinder M3 left its 1992 six cylinder successor such a tough task that BMW Motorsport was torn with internal discussions over whether to use the M3 badge at all. Having driven the latest showroom M3s, with their smooth 286 bhp from 3-litres, I can see why there was a strong lobby for the company to return to the honourable CSi suffix. Motorsport had genuinely developed the thoroughly uprated 3-series coupé from a 325i base to compete, so it was understandable that the commercially potent M-prefix remained on the rump.

Above
The magnificent M3 stole the hearts of those who previously thought the only four cylinder BMW for an enthusiast was an 02. The 195 bhp catalytic convertor M3 looked well inside and out. It sold extremely well, but there was a long delay before a successor was nominated for importation

Right
Bastos-sponsored 1992 M3. BMW M Power incarnate. See page 123 for further veiws of this warhorse

The BMW company tale is one of the most fascinating in automotive lore and the cars amongst the most consistently enjoyable, yet practical, in their chosen field.

I hope I have given you a taste of the fascination the marque can exert. Particularly so as BMW bounds forward with apparently unquenchable zest for making the most accessible of quality classics a matter of daily routine, as well as history.

The 2.5 litre Evolution Sport model of 1990 was developed in just six months and made in a big hurry before the Munich factory tooling for the E30 saloons was abandoned in favour of the current E36 manufacturing hardware. The 238 bhp road car was good for an honest 150 mph

This 2. 5 litre racer has an honourable history, being the factory backed M3 that led a
BMW 1–2 result in the 1992 Spa 24 hours for previous Spa winner Jean Michel
Martin of Belgium, Britain's Steve Soper and ex-Formula 1 BMW protegée, Christian
Danner. It is still owned by BMW in Munich, but is seen here on a goodwill mission at
Sebring, USA

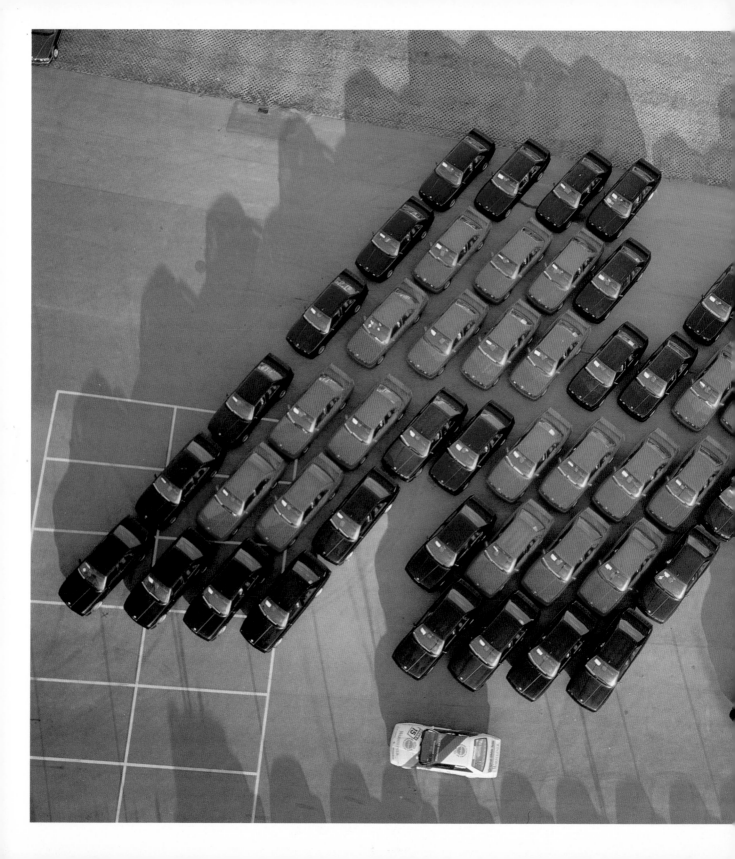

Above

The fastest M3 around the Nürburgring in its final (sixth) racing season was this 1992 M3 for Johnny Cecotto. It had major chassis engineering input from Simtek in Bicester, England and Michelin rubber on 18-inch wheel diameters. Here it is wheeled out to set pole position at that meeting, when it offered the only podium position BMW opposition to the Mercedes of Klaus Ludwig and former World Champion, Keke Rosberg

Left

How the last M3 homologation was won. The factory Evolution Sports line for a solemn counting ceremony and this colourful testimony to the M-badge in 1990

Above
Pure pleasure: the ex-Korman Autoworks M3 Firehawk contender is driven by Gary Davis at Sebring

Right
Despite filthy weather and a recalcitrant Ford camera car driven by the author, Malcolm Griffiths of LAT in London managed this fabulous picture of the dominant 1992 British Touring Car Championship equipe at a Brands Hatch test session. Steve Soper's 318iS is driven by the man himself whilst the grey 325i coupé kept him company in the hands of 1992 British Champion Tim Harvey. The pictures have not been seen before because the team owner of the period was having long term bother with the police; days later he was arrested and the pictures were filed away

Overleaf
3-Series for the 1990s. The success of the 'little' BMWs holds lessons for any marketing endeavour. The subtle styling evolution has worked. Quite simply, has any manufacturer in the world a better reputation for producing 'real' machines for grownups?